To anyone who could not put their
feelings to words,
This is for you.

HE

ME

...

Samantha Hope Boulgarides

This is my story,
You can never take it away from me.
You can mangle it,
Twist it,
Interpret it how you will,
Spit it out how you choose,
But know I was honest.
My words were truth.

   - Even if the truth was ugly
     (It is more often than not)

November 2015

THE BEGINNING

We stayed there, gazing endlessly into each other's eyes. He gently rose as I leaned down, his eyes pulling me in like gravity. He kissed me.

"I'm sorry."

"But why?"

"I don't want to be in a relationship."

"Oh...I understand."

I didn't understand.
I could hear him repeat "I'm sorry" as he retreated into my arms.
From this point on he knew, no matter what, I would always take him back.
I'd hate myself ten times worse if I let him go.

   - He was all I wanted

September 6, 2015

As the sky grows darker my thoughts burrow
deeper into my mind,
And with every yawn
           I fall farther
                      And farther
                                  In love with you.

Some truths are beautiful,
But those truths have a silver lining,
The lies we are told.

   - Or the lies we tell ourselves

July 23, 2016

We were lying down and I glanced over at this beautiful boy I had the privilege of calling mine.
He took a deep breath in as if he was trying to inhale an entire galaxy into his lungs.
I asked him…

"Why do you breathe so deeply?"

"Because it might be my last."

- 12:47 a.m.

I am caught in an endless cycle of lying to myself to feel okay.

   - I have never been okay

July 24, 2016

Why nourish a flower that will never grow,
Or grow into a weed?

- a lesson in friends or significant
  others

July 28, 2016

Every time I saw him perform I got a queasy feeling down at the bottom of my stomach, like I was watching something magical. I went weak at the knees and my heart thumped just thinking of him.

"I wonder if when he sees me, he feels the same way?"

A part of me knew I should never ask him, because I would only receive an answer I didn't want to hear. I would have to lie to myself, and that would hurt even worse.

July 28, 2016

I knew that if I kept holding on,
I'd end up wasting my entire life.

-I had to become stronger than my fear of
losing him.

August 6, 2016

Somewhere between loving him and hating myself,
I had decided that I was unworthy of anyone else's love besides his.
That this broken love was the grandest thing I would ever receive.

- Something is better than nothing

August 6, 2016

SHAME ON ME

I saw, I knew, I ignored.
I could no longer cry over him.
I could only cry over my own decision.
The decision I made to stay.

ABOVE OR BELOW

I always felt like I was the most important
thing in his life,
or the least.

   - Most times it was the latter

CONSISTENT

I could no longer play the victim.
I was completely aware of the situation.
I was completely aware that this boy was
consistent.
Consistent as the wax and wane of the moon.
Consistently treating me like I was
nothing.

WORDS

I always read things he has written for me, hoping it will make me feel better about our relationship. That after I read the things he wrote I will know he loves me, cares for me, and wishes he could be with me right now. But they're just words. Words mean nothing.

I feed off telling people horrible things he's done and then listening to them bash him, and tell me to break up with him.

In so many ways, it's everything I wish to tell myself.

Each day I decide whether or not I am worthy of your love.

I didn't hear from you so I guess that means "No."

July 28, 2016

"He never texts me."
"I never see him."
"A relationship shouldn't be this hard."
"Should I text him?"
"Why hasn't he texted?"
"He doesn't put any effort in"
"I'm sure he misses me!"
"He canceled our date again."
"I'm sure he's busy…"
"He's such a jerk."
"He never tells me I'm important to him."
"I'm always afraid he'll find someone better than me."
"He told me about a girl he really liked, but he promised he would try to abstain for me"
"I'm sure he didn't mean to come across that way."
"One person always has to try harder in relationships anyway."
"He only said it because I told him to…"
"I feel like I have to lure him into a conversation."
"I know I wasn't the only one he was saying goodnight to."
"I wonder if he thinks about her more than me."
"At least he was honest."
"He repeated her name in his journal."
"He wasn't jealous, he actually didn't care."
"I miss him."

"Break up with him, he doesn't deserve you."

"I know."

If she texted,
Would you leave her on "read"?
Or would you answer.

   - I get left on "read"

NOTHING

I didn't think it was possible to hold onto "nothing" until I was holding onto you.

- You are nothing to me.

ILLUSION OF LOVE

How can I miss what was never here?
You weren't here.
You never were.

im beginning to understand...

WAITING GAME

I know exactly what I want to hear come out
of your mouth.
I'm waiting.

   - You never say it.

You had a ripple effect on me, never ending.
Sometimes big, sometimes small.
But always there.

"you had a ripple effect on me. never ending, sometimes small, sometimes big, but always there." - HB

Shame on me,
Apparently, I was the only one dumb enough to believe this could work.

   - sorry for wasting your time

August 1, 2016

I text, and you respond.
I react as if you texted by your own
desire.
I love you.
You give me the attention I waved in front
of your face.

I text, you don't respond.
I text again saying I will never text first
again.
I hate you.
You still don't respond.

I hate myself for loving you, hating you,
then doing it all over again.

August 2, 2016

WHY

He asked me,

"Why? Why do you stay with me? What's there for you? I know why I'm staying, but why are you?"

I drew a blank.

- I guess that's a bad sign

August 4, 2016

WASTED WORDS

"Good night, I love you."

 "Good night, don't let the bedbugs bite."

I couldn't say I love you. Not this time.
I'd wasted so much time trying to have the
love I felt reciprocated, that when it
finally returned to me, I hadn't the desire
to say it back.

August 5, 2016

WHAT I'M MISSING

They told me I was,
"Missing something"
And that one day I would,
"Realize".
But I don't know what I'm missing,
or what I should be realizing,
"I know what I'm allowing him to do to me
is toxic".
But they said,
"It's bigger than that, but somehow so
small".

August 6, 2016

I'm so done saying sorry for your actions.
I'm so done thinking I was the one in the wrong.
I'm so done believing I could've done more.
I'm so done making up for what you lack.
It was never me.
It was always you.
Now it's your turn to clean up the mess.

- Your mess

August 6, 2016

Some part of me isn't afraid of losing you anymore.

I've been trying to find what ignites the
fire inside me, but how can it be the same
thing that put it out in the first place?

   - him

GHOST

Unless you were physically with me,
You were never there.
No texts.
No calls.
No comments.
I was dating a ghost.
So, no.
I am not in a relationship.

TRUE OR FALSE

I can't tell if I want things for the right reasons.
I can't tell if something happened one way or that's just how I remember it.
Are my intentions pure?
Am I lying to myself?
Where did the truths end, and lies begin?

   - Or was it all lies in the first place?

CRIME AND PUNISHMENT

When he was gone, we did the same thing.
We fell for other people.

He told me about a girl.
He repeated her name in his journal.
He said she was second best.

I told him about a boy.
I told him he was just alright.

I didn't tell him that
He made me feel important and loved.
I held my tongue.

I felt guilty.
I apologized.
He never apologized.

Why am I punishing myself?
It was the same crime.

US VS. THEM

How come when it comes to ourselves,
All our opinions and standards change?
That when our friends need advice we always
say that no matter what, they deserve the
world and should expect more.

But when it comes to our own needs, we feel
like we're being greedy and should be
content with what we are given. That
somehow our own self-worth is far lesser
than that of the people around us.

Happiness is not synonymous with settling.

I feel like every time you left I had to press the restart button.
No matter how perfect or horrible the experience had been, all the time in between was used for me to decide whether or not I still loved you.

   - Do I love him?
       Do I love him not?

August 7, 2016

THE CHEATER AND THE CHEATED

There is some part of me that wants to cheat.
Just to see them come back to me.
They would still love me.
They would be down on their knees.
I could do no wrong in their eyes.
Because no matter what,
All they would want is me.

I hate myself for wanting this.

But I'm tired of being on my knees.

You *NEVER* deserved this much of me.

"You never deserved this much of me.
you never deserved this much
of me. —HB 9-16

August 7, 2016

NOTHING LEFT

"Please dump him and save yourself the tears."

"*I don't think I've saved any part of myself by dating him.*"

GIRL WHO CRIED WOLF

I've threatened to break up with him so many times. I don't even believe myself anymore.

-1000 times

August 9, 2016

BEGINNING OF THE END

God, care about something for once! Just feel something, you've been numb to me for so long. Are you even breathing?

- 2:57 p.m.

August 9, 2016

Words may come off beautiful, but most times they come from a place of great pain. Because nothing ends poetically. We are just re-writing our stories. It makes them easier to swallow.

HIM

The idea of him used to leave me
breathless, warm. I used to treasure the
days where he and I were one.

But now the thought makes my stomach turn.
The only thing his fingers could bring me
is poison,
And the only thing they could retrieve is
pain.

I wonder what it will be like to see him again.
Will it be different?
Will we see each other and feel hate?
Maybe it will be like all the movies where they suddenly remember they're soulmates.
What if I don't say "hi" first, and we don't talk at all?
What if he assumes it's already over?
Do I let it be?
Do I fight?
Or have I already fought,
And lost the battle?

You said didn't mean to hurt me,
But you did.

    - I think you meant to

NOT YOURS

I don't want to give him power over me, but it's hard to be your own person when you've been "his" for so long.

```
He does this every time.
He steps on my heart,
He makes me cry.
```

August 11, 2016

						It will be ok
						   //
						You will be ok

it will be ok.
i will be ok.

Maybe,
Expectations were meant to be broken.

August 11, 2016

COMMUNICATION

I don't think what I want from him is wrong,
Is it?

Someone had told me that when you don't feel obligated to talk to someone, it makes a relationship "stress free".

But shouldn't a relationship be the mutual care, respect, and communication between two people?

Isn't that the foundation for any good relationship?

August 11, 2016

"Enjoy just knowing you're dating him. He's a catch. Be proud. Sport that like a medal."

        "But I'm also a catch?! I shouldn't be more proud of him, than I am of myself."

Like I should be content just knowing I share a label with him. I shouldn't be proud of dating someone who makes me second guess my own worth.

- People are not medals
    Especially him

My dad always said no one can **make** you feel anything.

Maybe I wanted to get hurt.

August 13, 2016

I see his name everywhere

- John

MISSING PIECE

Maybe I gave him too much of me
And now I can't continue on my own.

LEAVING

I should be able to walk away.
I will find someone better, someday.

   - It's easier said than done

I chose to let you hurt me.

(Why do I keep blaming myself?)

August 13, 2016

MY DOING

Regardless of what he does
I need to take responsibility for my own actions.
I knew what I was receiving,
Sometimes I was ok with it,
And sometimes I wasn't.
When I wasn't, I made it hell on earth.
I forced misery on both of us.

August 14, 2016

Seeking comfort in the arms of others is dangerous.
Because after a while you forget you have arms of your own.

You are the reason I know I'm strong enough.

Thank you.

August 14, 2016

TEMPORARY

Some people say they want everything to last forever.
But I can tell you right now that's a lie.
Temporary is better than forever.
Because forever is more of a curse than it is a blessing.
Forever stands in the way of change and change stands in the way of progress and without progress nothing that should've happened will happen.
Because happiness is just as temporary as pain.
And I can bet you,
Right now,
As you lay crying for him,
You couldn't be happier for temporary.

STAND UP FOR YOURSELF

There comes a time when you can no longer
allow yourself to be the only one
contributing to a relationship.

August 15, 2016

HE'S GONE

Moving on is hard when they are everywhere.
In people walking on the street.
In names of restaurants.
In places you go.
In stories you tell.
In memories you have.
In every single inch of your body.
Because he was once there.
With his hands.
With his lips.
With his heart and soul.

He was once there.
And now he's not.

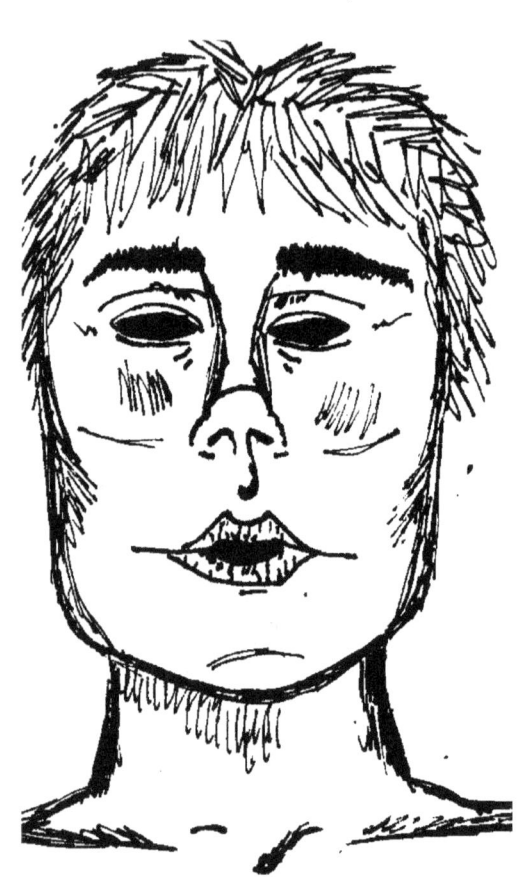

SNAP

You can only settle for so long.
One day you will wake up,
Realize what everyone has been telling you,
And be done.
You will have put your foot down.
Enough is enough.
This will be the most painful and
liberating day of your life.

I know what I'm doing.
I'm making it easier for you to leave.
Because if you leave,
Then I have to.

August 16, 2016

GIVERS AND TAKERS

If you assume pouring yourself into someone
will somehow result in receiving their
affection,
You are wrong.
People like him will take what they want
never offering something in return.

- Stop giving yourself to him.
He doesn't deserve you.

LOVE

Sink or swim.
Heaven or hell.
Light or dark.

There is no middle ground.

Forcing things to work,
And things actually working are two
different things.

August 16, 2016

No matter how much you want him to be the one,
He will never be the one.

- People don't change

August 17, 2016

My heart dropped,
Of course it was her.
Of course he was kissing her.
Hands around her waist,
Lips pressed against her.
Why did I trust him?

But could I expect any less?

He said nothing happened.
That was a *lie*.

August 17, 2016

Everything they told me about him was true.
They were all right.
He doesn't deserve the cruel things I have to say.
He would get the satisfaction of knowing I care.

August 17, 2016

"I thought trust was enough..."

"You lied about cheating on me. Don't you lecture me about *trust*."

August 18, 2016

HIS ABSENCE

The day after is always the hardest.
Because you rack your brain with any
reason, any explanation to why he didn't
stay. You begin to think it was you, that
you weren't good enough. That you didn't
give him enough of you. As if there was
something more you could've done to stop
him from leaving.
But that's the thing, it wasn't you. It was
never you. It was him. He left you, and you
deserve someone who doesn't leave that
easy.

I thought he was going to change.
I thought I could change him.
I thought I'd be his last.

   - how could I be so ignorant

once a cheater
///
always a cheater

August 19, 2016

How could he cheat, and blame me for portraying him badly? I was the one who was stabbed in the back, not him.
All I did was reveal the truth.

I hope your bed of lies is comfortable.

To the girl after me:

Beware. All evil things disguise themselves as something beautiful. You will never be treated the way you deserve. He sits back and watches you run circles around him... It makes him feel powerful.

I never meant that much to you…

Too bad I'm realizing this now.

To hell with closure.

Nothing you say could make me change my mind.
I hope you suffer.

I don't get how he could treat me like this,

And I can still miss him.

He never said "*sorry*".

August 20, 2016

FIRST STAGE OF GRIEF

This is denial.
Where I think I'm going to wake up and
everything will be different.
But it won't.

   — I need to come to terms with reality.

I will never deny myself emotions,
But I will never let you see.

You should be flattered by the fact I
trusted you so much.
You should be flattered that I didn't think
you could do something like this.
You should be flattered because I thought
you were a far better person than who you
turned out to be.

You are the only person who can realize
your worth.

He will regret it one day.
He will never find someone who loved his flaws the way I did.

- I won't regret leaving

August 20, 2016

I think it all feels the same,
Before and after your first kiss.
Maybe mentally something has changed,
But my lips feel just as cold.

August 25, 2016

Nothing was more real than the moment he said,

"I guess I can because I'm single now."

You could have buried me right there. My skin was crawling, my heart rose to my throat.

- How could he have moved on so quickly?

There's a fine line between *compromising* and *settling.*

GETTING OVER YOU

This will be the hardest things I have ever done.

August 25, 2016

It's hard to wake up every morning and see you.
You used to be my reason for waking up.
I used to run into your arms.
Now I can't even look at you.

What good does it do to run back into the arms that broke you?

EVERYTHING CHANGES

Everything is until it isn't.
Everyone can until they can't.
We all will until we won't.

This isn't love anymore.
I can't love you.
And we won't ever be the same.

The day he told me he loved me, was the most beautiful day. His words tasted like cinnamon, and felt like silk. But the day he left, it was the opposite. It tasted like acid and felt like flames. It split me in two, now I'm numb.

I've forgot how many days it's been, but it hasn't gotten any easier. Every moment I'm thinking about him. When I'm alone, my insides split in two, my ribs break and I'm clutching my chest in a futile act of trying to keep from falling apart.

Heart break is putting it lightly, because this isn't breaking, it's ripping, it's tearing, it's burning, it's losing every single thing about yourself to a battle you've already lost.

- I don't think I've stopped crying.

August 25, 2016

No matter how much you want to forget someone, how much you want to forget *him*. You can't. You can realize that he's not the right person for you, and you can realize that he is nothing but toxic. But he was a person in your life and he was a very important one, he made you feel. And someone like that isn't so easy to forget.

August 25, 2016

There are no good days anymore,
Just bad days,
And worse ones.

August 25, 2016

I settled,
Compromised my own worth,
And I still wasn't enough for you.

August 27, 2016

You'd think, with all the sad stories I tell, that I would've realized sooner that this thing I called love, was anything but. But I didn't realize it, and I regret all the time I wasted on him. I regret all the time I hated myself because of him. But I do not regret all the lessons I learned and all the strength I gained.

I am more than worthy of love.

He had no love to give.

August 27, 2016

I think if someone leaves you, and causes you pain, they should give you the courtesy of staying gone. Because it is even crueler to come back into someone's life and expect to be loved the same way.

If you're going to leave,
Never come back.

August 27, 2016

Billions of people feel heartbreak,
But still feel alone.
Like it's the end,
And there is nothing left beyond that one person.
As if the best part of life has already flashed before our eyes.
You had the privilege of loving someone with your whole heart,
You loved someone till it physically hurt.
It's their loss if they didn't feel the same way.
And in however long,
6 months,
A year,
You will forget this pain that seems so endless,
And fall in love all over again.

I shouldn't have to make you stay.
If you want to leave, then go. I'm not
stopping you.

    - Not this time

I never expected to feel this way. To feel
this hurt in every limb of my body, because
I know he doesn't love me.

    - Not anymore

August 29, 2016

One lie from you caused more damage than 15 years of self-hatred ever could.

If they wanted to stay,
They'd stay.
There's nothing you could've done.
You deserve someone who doesn't leave that easily.

   - I'm sorry

REGRET

I wonder how he feels knowing he lost someone who loved him more than all the stars in the sky. Someone who would've walked miles just to be there for him, someone who put his need above their own. I wonder what that type of regret must feel like.

August 30, 2016

No one really notices until it begins to
fall apart,
And in no time at all,
You're holding the ashes in the palms of
your hands.

August 31, 2016

It's rare to find anything beautiful in life that lasts half as long as you'd like it too.

August 31, 2016

There was time when we actually said what we meant. But now we throw around words giving them no weight or meaning.
When did "I love you" become another word for "goodbye"?

August 31, 2016

BE CAREFUL WHAT YOU WISH FOR

It's so strange to want something for so long,
Finally have it,
Then realize it's not what you want.
It's becomes more elusive than it was at the start.

September 2, 2016

KARMA

I hope that one day, it all gets back to you. The lies, the other girls, the broken promises, the times you hurt me. When it does, I hope to see the ruin you become. I hope I see the tears you cry, the blood you bleed. I hope life pours salt in your wounds and shoots daggers in your eyes.

There are men who will not treat you with such cruelty, do not let him make you cynical.

September 2, 2016

It's interesting how you flew across the country to see her, but never crossed a freeway to see me.

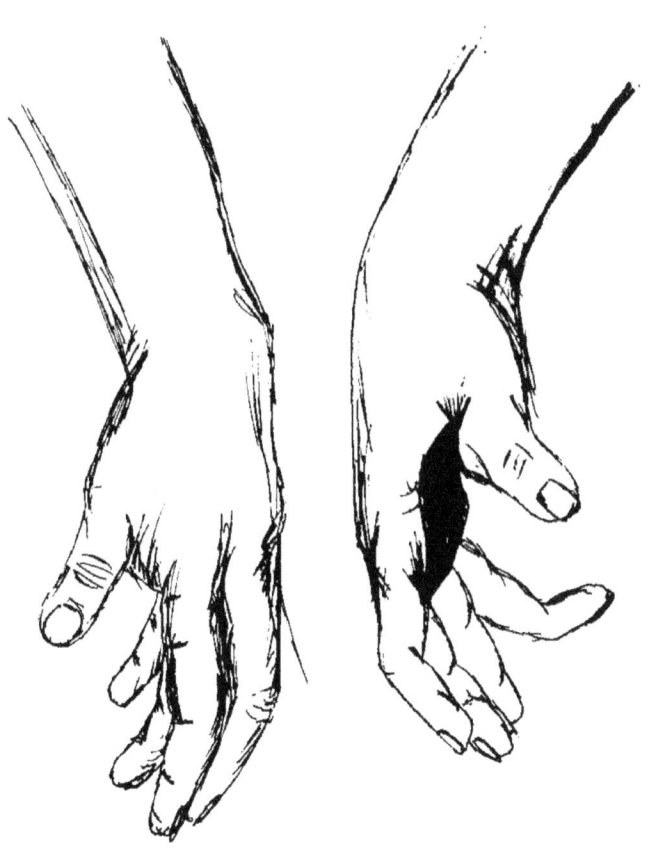

September 3, 2016

Your words never matched your actions.
What you fed me daily was a facade to keep
me from walking away.
I can flashback to all the times you used
my vulnerability as your strength.
All the words, all the letters,
You knew exactly what to say
And when to say it.
You're a master of disguise
who played me like a puppet.

September 3, 2016

In a way, this is all a blessing.
Blessings hurt sometimes.
If I wasn't hurting now,
I would be hurting ten times worse later.
If I didn't find out the way I did,
At the time I did,
I'd still be with him.
Settling,
And sacrificing,
For someone who never really cared.

September 4, 2016

I had a dream about him.
He asked for my forgiveness,
then kissed me till I melted into my shoes.
I told him I knew more than he thought,
About her,
About him.
He got angry and I remembered why I left.
Some part of me wanted to stay.
But a kiss,
And moment,
A temporary feeling,
Is no reason to stay.

September 5, 2016

In good conscience, I can't say that love hurts. Because love never hurt. Love that you never gave, and the love I never received, hurt.

September 5, 2016

What an interesting and rewarding concept
it is to belong solely to yourself.

I BELONG DEEPLY TO MYSELF

September 6, 2016

Sometimes I imagine all the girls you have touched, just like me. All the girls you will touch, just like me. The way they will give themselves to you, just like I did. You will feed them lies and whisper sweet nothings into their ears, gently inching them closer and closer to the edge. And after you push, you'll never look back.

September 8, 2016

He has a trick of picking the silent ones.
The ones who can't stand up for themselves.
But I won't be silent.
I will make a ruckus of the ruin you've made.
You won't get away with it.

September 8, 2016

I could've looked at you for hours and found a million things I loved just between your smile and the bridge of your nose. I saw universes in your eyes and I loved it all.

You never looked at me that way. Maybe you were scared of falling too deep, or maybe you knew I deserved everything you couldn't give me.

September 14, 2016

WHEN THE RAIN DOESN'T FALL

The rain does not fall anymore, but the clouds still grow.

The sky still turns darker and darker and darker, but there is no relief.

No exhale after the inhale.

This sadness does not make me cry anymore, but I wish it did.

I'd prefer tears over whatever this pain is.

September 14, 2016

I want to be able to kiss someone without feeling you on my lips. I want to be able to walk down a hallway without remembering all the times you walked with me. I want to live for me and not for you. I don't want you to be my sun. I am the sun, you revolve around me.

September 14, 2016

He had his cake and ate it too.
But he left the crumbs for me.

- Crumbs were enough to keep me loving him

September 14, 2014

I crave you.
I'm licking you off my fingertips,
Cleaning my plate of crumbs.

   - I'm still hungry

September 14, 2014

How can our mind be our own worst enemy?

September 14, 2016

STUCK ON THE PAST

It makes me sad that there are things in my life I will have only have done with him. The moment came and passed just as quickly as our love did. I thought I had appreciated it all while it was here, but I guess not. I'm still finding little moments I forgot we ever had. But there's no point in remembering these things now. There is no WE. These memories, these feelings, they need to stop. I need to move on. Just like he did all that time ago...

September 14, 2016

DUST TO DUST

The more the waves hit the shore, the smaller the rocks become.
Until rocks become sand, and from sand to dust swept away by the wind.

Maybe talking about you is like the rocks, and eventually the way I feel will turn to dust.

September 15, 2016

I don't want to be rude but unless you're,

"I'm sorry"

Can undo what he did,
I'm afraid you're not helping.

    - If I can't help myself
               You certainly can't

September 15, 2016

PERCEPTION

What I see in you,
And what you see in me,
Is completely different than what they see.
I look at you and you look at me,
And everyone else is on the outside looking in.
Perception.
What I saw then and what I see now,
Is completely different.
Now you are looking at her and she's looking at you,
And I am on the outside looking in.

September 15, 2016

We are rocks crashing on the shore, ever changing by the way the waves hit.

September 15, 2016

Some people find it easier to let go...
Some people find it easier to hold on...

... You always preferred letting go.

EXPLANATIONS

Everyone needs an explanation.
No one can handle the idea that for no reason,
Out of the blue,
Everything changed.
Maybe it was something you did,
Or maybe it wasn't.
Either way you need to know why they do not love you anymore.
And even if he tells you,
You will never stop wondering why you weren't enough for him.

September 16, 2016

How come he and I are the only two people
who can't realize my worth?
The only person I want to realize,
And only person that should realize,
Don't.
How ironic is that?

September 16, 2016

Let's be real for a second...

You treated me like shit.

September 16, 2016

Just hearing your name gives me anxiety.
People shouldn't have the power to do that.
I shouldn't give you that power. But I do,
and it feels like I have no control over
the simplest things anymore. I don't know
how to make this stop, but I wish I did.

September 16, 2016

ALONE

I mean I get it, cheating seems like a good idea at the time. You're somewhere else, away from the person you originally said you'd love. That new person seems so beautifully exciting. You think that maybe you didn't love that person back home. So, you throw that all away and have a little fun. But when you come back you expect that original person to still love you, even though you stopped loving them. But they don't love you anymore. Now you're lonely again, but this time you don't have them. You don't have anyone. I guess that's the problem, isn't it, you just assume people constantly want you, so you continue to throw away people that matter. You use everyone until there's no one else left to use. Then, you're right back where you started. *Alone*.

You know what, I take that back. I don't understand how you can cheat knowing you hold someone else's heart in your hands.

September 17, 2016

People change and that's ok.
We may be a good fit today,
but maybe not tomorrow.
I'm okay if you need to leave to have more
room to grow,
I understand.
But give me a fair warning.
I don't want to wake up one day to see
you've left and are never coming back.
If you have the courage to leave,
have the courage to tell me.

September 17, 2016

You can't move on without acknowledging the past.

September 18, 2016

Don't whine about something you can change. Don't pretend to be helpless when you're not.

September 18, 2016

How come everyone finds it so easy to leave when all I ever wanted was for them to stay?

- It's like I'm the only one who hates to see people walk away.

September 19, 2016

There are certain things in life apologies can't fix.

This was one of them.

September 19, 2016

YOU'RE ABSENCE

Now that you're gone for good, I guess I can truly say my heart feels just as empty as when you were here.

September 23, 2016

Unless you yourself have drowned in his blood, do not judge me for cursing his name with my every breath.

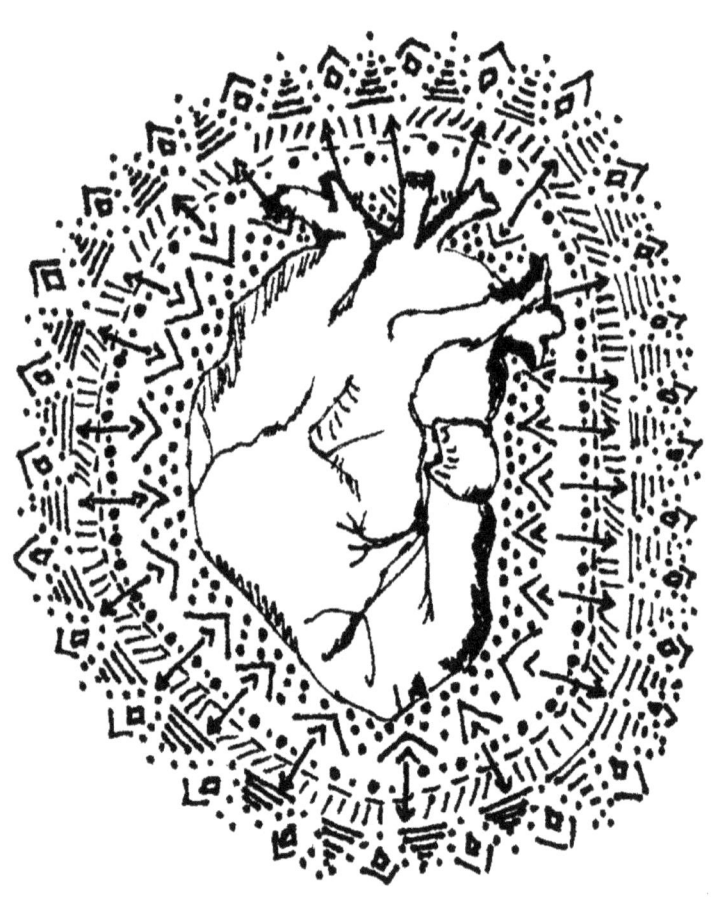

September 23, 2016

One day you will love like I loved,
And then you will hurt like I hurt.
Only then will you understand how your entire universe can revolve around one person.

So for now, don't judge my pain based on your happiness. I used to be happy too.

September 25, 2016

I wonder how long it will be till I feel
for someone the same way I felt for you.

September 29, 2016

I will be the love I never received.

This began and ended with his lips.

His lips kissing me.

And his lips kissing her.

October 2, 2016

If you need to wonder whether or not you have moved on, truth is, you probably haven't.

I am okay.
Actually,
I am better than okay,
I'm amazing.
Yes, I'm sure some days will be harder than others,
And I will resent you,
But I don't need you.
I never did.
My life will be that much more beautiful now that you're gone.

October 4, 2016

I am not afraid to have you read this, in fact, I hope you do. I was weak, incapable of seeing the good in myself and the flaws in you. But I am awake now. Because of you I now demand congruency, love, and respect in all relationships. You were a lesson I needed to learn. Thank you.

I'm closing this chapter, promising myself
I will no longer dedicate any more pages to
someone like you.

You have reached the end, thank you. It brings me peace to have my voice be heard and to have you, my beloved reader, know that not everyone will treat you the way you deserve, but that does not mean you deserve any less. It is inevitable in life that we encounter people who will only see us only as objects they can use. Sometimes we fall in their trap and it will be hard to get out, but you can. You can overcome anything. We must strive to only allow people into our lives who will treat us with kindness and congruency, we must also treat others with that same kindness.

Don't forget to love yourself,
you deserve that.
You come before anyone else.

Love,

Samantha

Hope

Boulgarides

ABOUT THE AUTHOR

Samantha Hope Boulgarides was born and lives in Southern California. Growing up, Samantha utilized the arts as an outlet for self-expression and personal discovery. She began using writing as an outlet at the age of 13 in response to hardships in her personal life. During her first significant relationship, Samantha began using sketching and poetry to record the life changing experience. This process would become her first book, He over Me. Samantha currently studies at the Orange County School of the Arts.

www.ingramcontent.com/pod-product-compliance
Lightning Source LLC
Chambersburg PA
CBHW061324040426
42444CB00011B/2764